QUEEN ELIZABETH I

LEON ASHWORTH

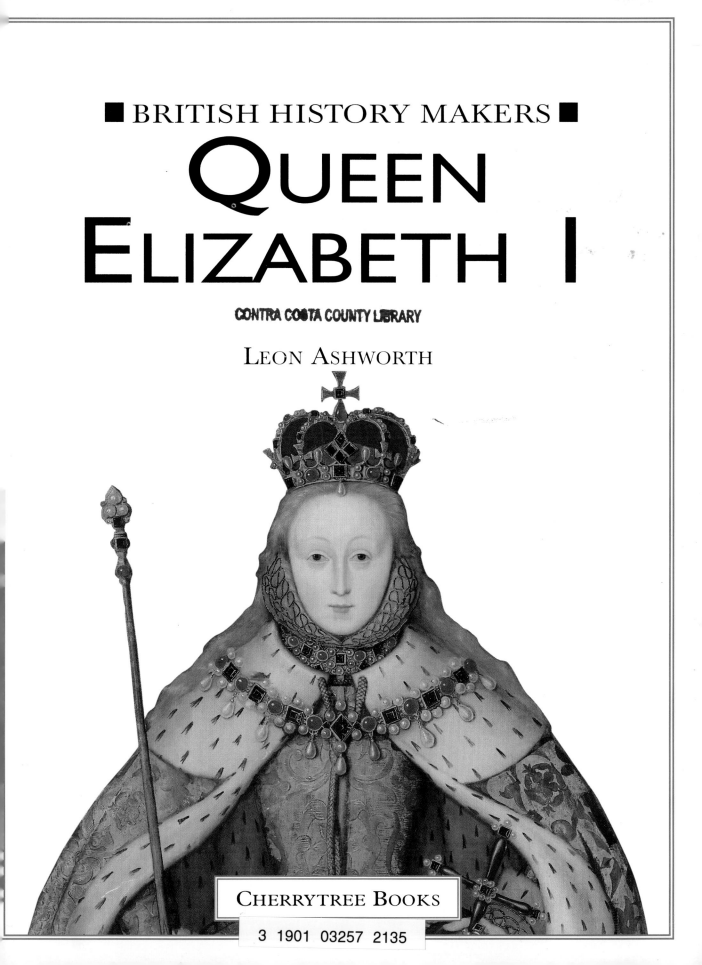

CHERRYTREE BOOKS

A Cherrytree Book

Designed and produced by
A S Publishing

First published 2002
by Cherrytree Press
327 High Street
Slough
Berkshire
SL1 1TX

British Library Cataloguing in Publication Data

Ashworth, Leon
   Elizabeth I. – (British history makers)
   1.Elizabeth, I, Queen of England, 1533-1603, Queen of Great
   Britain
   2.Queens – England
   3.Great Britain – History – Elizabeth, 1558-1603
   I.Title
   942'.055'092

ISBN 1 84234 071 9

Acknowledgments
Design: Richard Rowan
Editorial: John Collins
Artwork: Gwen Green
Consultant: Brian Williams
Photographs: *AKG London* 5, 11 bottom, 14 top, 15 bottom, 16
bottom (& cover), 17 left top and centre, 19 centre, 20 top
and bottom, 21 left centre and bottom right, 22 top,
22/23 (& back cover), 25 bottom, 27 bottom right, 28/29
bottom; *The Art Archive* 2 top left (& 9 top right), 3 top right
(& 15 top), 4 top and centre, 6 top, 7 top left, top right and
bottom, 9 bottom, 11 top right, 15 centre, 16 top, 17 right,
18 top and bottom left, 18/19 bottom, 19 top left, 21 top
and centre, 24 centre and bottom; *The Bridgeman Art
Library* 2 bottom left (& 12 bottom), 11 top left; *Britain on
View* 13 bottom right, 28 top; *Mary Evans Picture Library*
12 top, 19 right, 27 top; *National Maritime Museum,
London* 6 bottom; *National Portrait Gallery* 1 (& 14), 2
bottom right (& 10), 7 left centre, 8 top, 9 top left,
10, 11 left centre and bottom, 13 left centre, 26;
Royal Collection Picture Library 8 (& cover portrait).

CONTENTS

■ QUEEN FOR AN AGE ■

ELIZABETH I was the last of England's great Tudor monarchs. She was the queen who never married, who roused her people to fight the might of the Spanish Armada, and who gave her name to an age – the Elizabethan age.

Elizabeth was much like her father, King Henry VIII. She had energy, intelligence, stubbornness and a furious temper when anyone dared oppose her. She reigned at a time of great change in England. The Renaissance had brought new ideas in art and science. The Reformation had changed religion and the church.

During Elizabeth's lifetime the world also changed, as European explorers sailed across the ocean to North and South America. England grew more powerful through its navy, and more self-confident. This was an age of dash and daring, of bold sailors like Francis Drake, and of poets like William Shakespeare, the greatest of all English writers. In everything she did, Elizabeth was helped by her chosen advisers, especially William Cecil who was made Lord Burghley in 1571.

Elizabeth enjoyed a long reign, despite many threats to her safety. When she became queen, England faced danger from foreign enemies and was divided at home by religion. When she died, she left a united country that believed in itself, and was richer than ever before.

ELIZABETH'S LIFE

1533 Born.
1536 Her mother, Anne Boleyn, executed.
1558 Becomes queen after the death of her sister Mary I.
1577 Drake sails around the world.
1587 Mary Queen of Scots is executed on Elizabeth's orders.
1588 Defeat of the Spanish Armada saves England from invasion.
1603 Dies.

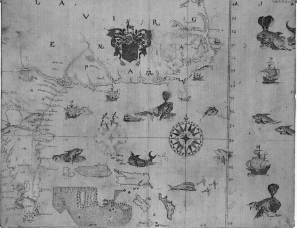

▲ England's power and wealth depended on the sea. Her father's great ship, the *Mary Rose* (top) sank when Elizabeth was 12. As queen, Elizabeth sent ships to find new trade and new lands, like Virginia (above) in North America. Her daring sailors raided Spain's galleons and defeated its Armada.

▼ Elizabeth's signature was as stylish and extravagant as her dress.

'I will have here but one mistress and no master' Elizabeth warned her would-be husband Robert Dudley, Earl of Leicester.

She is *'much attached to the people and is very confident that they take her part'* said the Spanish ambassador when Elizabeth became queen in 1558.

'I have but the body of a weak and feeble woman, but I have the heart and stomach of a king.' Elizabeth speaking to her soldiers at Tilbury in 1588.

◀ **A portrait of Elizabeth, painted by Marcus Geeraerts in 1588, the year of the Armada.**

■ THIRD IN LINE ■

ELIZABETH'S mother was Anne Boleyn, the second of Henry VIII's six wives. His first wife, Catherine of Aragon, had given birth to a daughter, called Mary, in 1516, but was unable to have any more children. Henry was desperate for a son to succeed him. So, in 1533, he divorced Catherine to marry Anne. At the time, the church did not normally allow divorce, even for kings, except in special circumstances. The divorce caused a serious crisis between Henry and the leader of the church, the pope, in Rome.

EVENTS

1533 Thomas Cranmer is England's first Protestant archbishop of Canterbury. Pizzarro's Spanish army conquers the Incas of Peru.
1534 Henry VIII makes himself Supreme Head of the Church in England.
1535 Sir Thomas More is executed for defying Henry. Jacques Cartier of France explores St Lawrence river in Canada.
1536 Anne Boleyn is put to death. Henry begins to strip England's monasteries of their wealth.

A DAUGHTER, NOT A SON

Elizabeth was born in Greenwich Palace, near London. The king was sure that the baby would be a boy, and had planned a tournament to celebrate the event. The birth of a little girl on 7 September 1533 disappointed everyone. The celebrations were cancelled, and the baby's baptism was a fairly quiet affair. The child was named Elizabeth, after her grandmother, Elizabeth of York.

When she was only three months old, Elizabeth was taken away from her mother to live in a palace at Hatfield. Her 13-year-old sister Mary joined her. No longer called 'princess', because of her mother's divorce, Mary gave a frosty welcome to her little half-sister who had the grand title of Princess of England. Henry began planning a marriage for his new daughter, having his eye on a French prince. Marrying her to an ally would be the best way she could help strengthen his kingdom. What he really wanted, however, was a son. When Anne Boleyn failed to give him one, he turned elsewhere.

▲ Henry VII, Elizabeth's grandfather, was the first Tudor monarch. He was keen for English navigators to discover new lands.

▼ Greenwich Palace, where Elizabeth, like her father, was born. It was demolished in 1662.

▲ Henry VIII was not brought up to be king, for he had an older brother, Arthur. When Arthur died, Henry became king and married his brother's widow, Catherine of Aragon, the first of his six wives.

~ ELIZABETH I's FAMILY TREE ~

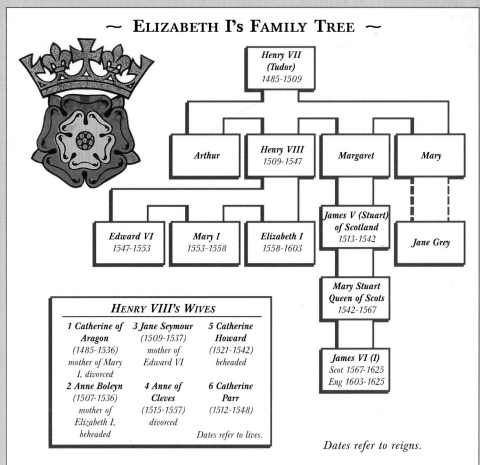

Henry VII (Tudor) 1485-1509

Arthur

Henry VIII 1509-1547

Margaret

Mary

Edward VI 1547-1553

Mary I 1553-1558

Elizabeth I 1558-1603

James V (Stuart) of Scotland 1513-1542

Jane Grey

Mary Stuart Queen of Scots 1542-1567

James VI (I) Scot 1567-1625 Eng 1603-1625

HENRY VIII'S WIVES		
1 Catherine of Aragon (1485-1536) mother of Mary I, divorced	3 Jane Seymour (1509-1537) mother of Edward VI	5 Catherine Howard (1521-1542) beheaded
2 Anne Boleyn (1507-1536) mother of Elizabeth I, beheaded	4 Anne of Cleves (1515-1557) divorced	6 Catherine Parr (1512-1548)
		Dates refer to lives.

Dates refer to reigns.

▲ Anne Boleyn's head was struck off by a swordsman sent from France. Elizabeth took care to speak of her mother only in private, but she kept her portrait in a special ring, and took as her own Anne's family motto: *'Always the same'*.

ELIZABETH LOSES HER MOTHER

On 2 May 1536 Anne was taken to the Tower of London. She was accused of treason, for being unfaithful to the king. Elizabeth, not yet three years old, never saw her mother again. On 19 May, Anne was beheaded.

LIFE IN TOWN AND COUNTRY

AFTER the long civil wars, known as the Wars of the Roses, ended in 1485, Tudor rule had brought peace and prosperity. Many people in England were farmers. Others worked in the growing towns, of which the biggest by far was London. Most towns and villages were tiny by comparison. There were beggars in the street, and poor people sleeping rough by the roadside, but most English people were better off than their grandparents. Noblemen lived in fine homes, and loved to go out to hunt with falcons.

■ SISTER TO THE KING ■

HENRY'S NEW wife was Jane Seymour, who gave birth to the son he longed for before dying 12 days later. The baby, Prince Edward, would be the next king of England.

Henry had no more interest in Elizabeth. Now that her mother was disgraced and dead, she was declared illegitimate. It seemed unlikely that this slim, red-haired girl would ever play much part in England's affairs, and certainly not as queen.

None the less, both the king's daughters were well educated. But there was one big difference between them. Elizabeth was brought up as a Protestant, not as a Catholic like her sister Mary. Her first teacher was Catherine 'Kat' Ashley, who gave her lessons in reading, writing and Latin, the language of scholars, government and the church.

EVENTS

1536 Henry VIII marries Jane Seymour.
1537 Jane gives birth to Henry's son, Edward.
1538 From now on by law, people in England have to register births, deaths and marriages.
1540 Henry marries Anne of Cleves, but soon divorces her and marries Catherine Howard, who is executed in 1542.
1542 English army defeats Scots invaders at battle of Solway Moss.
1543 Polish astronomer Copernicus states that the earth moves around the sun.
1545 Warship Mary Rose sinks, while preparing to fight the French. Council of Trent plans reform of the Roman Catholic Church.
1547 Henry VIII dies and Edward VI becomes king.

A SUCCESSION OF QUEENS

Elizabeth saw little of her father. Henry was busy marrying. He took two wives in 1540; first and very briefly Anne of Cleves and then Catherine Howard, whose head was cut off in 1542. Elizabeth was taken

▲ Catherine Parr was an excellent step-mother, well educated and clever. She helped Elizabeth with her studies.

◀ At the news of her father's death the 13-year-old Elizabeth wept briefly, but quickly recovered.

GOING TO SCHOOL

FEW girls in Tudor England had the kind of education Elizabeth so enjoyed. Books were too expensive for most families, and few poor children went to school. Other parents paid a private teacher, or tutor, to teach their children at home. Some boys went to grammar schools. Teachers often beat their pupils, but Prince Edward was lucky – his tutors were not allowed to beat the future king of England. An unlucky 'whipping boy' took the beatings instead.

▶ Only the rich could afford books, many of which, like this one, were still copied by hand, even though printing had been invented.

▲ Edward VI, the new king, wrote to Elizabeth telling her how much he admired her courage, 'because from your learning, you know what you ought to do'.

▶ Elizabeth loved to ride a horse, hunt, hawk and shoot a bow, like her father in his youth.

to court to welcome Anne, and was given some jewellery by Catherine, but was otherwise kept out of the way. Henry married for the last time in 1543. His sixth wife was Catherine Parr.

A FAST LEARNER

Catherine Parr saw to the children's education at Whitehall Palace in London. Elizabeth shared some lessons with her brother Edward, but from 1544 she had her own tutor, William Grindal. She was a clever child who soon spoke fluently in French and Italian, and could read and write Latin better than her father.

Prince Edward was being prepared for the day when he would be king. That day came on 28 January 1547, when Henry VIII died.

■ PRINCESS IN DANGER ■

EDWARD, AGED nine, was too young to rule alone. Among the nobles who jostled for power as advisers were his ambitious uncles, Edward and Thomas Seymour. Edward became the king's Protector. Thomas was jealous, but had plans of his own.

LEARNING LIFE'S LESSONS

Elizabeth was living in Chelsea with her step-mother Queen Catherine and Mrs Ashley. Thomas Seymour came there to court Catherine and the couple married in secret. Elizabeth was amused by her new 'uncle's' high-spirited games, but Catherine was not. Her husband was paying too much attention to the young girl. So she sent Elizabeth away to Hertfordshire.

Mr Grindal, Elizabeth's old teacher, had died of plague. Now she had a clever new tutor, Roger Ascham. The princess read books, played music on the lute and virginals, rode horses and hunted in the forests. She was safer away from the power games played out in London.

Thomas Seymour was playing a dangerous game. After his wife died, he resumed his flirtation with Elizabeth. In 1549 he was arrested and executed on a charge of treason. Mrs Ashley was dragged off to the Tower of London, and Elizabeth was questioned about her part in Seymour's scheming. She kept calm throughout the nerve-racking ordeal, demanding Mrs Ashley's freedom.

▶ Edward VI's health was always poor, and he lived for only six years after his coronation.

▲ Edward Seymour, duke of Somerset, was England's king in all but name. He ruled wisely on his nephew's behalf, but was executed in 1552.

▲ Tudor noblemen built large, elegant houses, some of which are still lived in today. They often had wood panels on the walls and solid oak tables, chairs and chests.

POWER POLITICS

Within three years, the elder Seymour had also lost his head and the boy-king Edward had a new Protector in the duke of Northumberland. Elizabeth had learned how deadly dangerous power politics could be. She now had some land of her own, left to her in her father's will. She managed the business herself, checking and signing each page in the account book.

▲ According to Elizabeth, Thomas Seymour was a 'man of much wit and little judgement'. She was clearly attracted to him, despite his age.

TUDOR ENTERTAINMENT

THE Tudors enjoyed a good time, though some of their sports we now think cruel, such as cock-fights and setting dogs to fight a chained bear. Nobles dressed up in armour for tournaments, trying their skill with sword and lance, and shooting arrows at targets. Gentlemen and ladies rode out on horses, for a day's hunting or hawking. People loved to sing and dance, especially at feasts and parties. The lute (right) and the flute (left) were popular instruments in Elizabeth's day. Country people thronged to watch actors, jugglers, fire-eaters and acrobats who travelled from one market town to the next.

■ SISTER TO THE QUEEN ■

BY 1553, YOUNG King Edward was dying, probably from tuberculosis. The duke of Northumberland plotted to put his daughter-in-law, Lady Jane Grey, on the throne but news leaked out and the people rallied to Princess Mary. When Edward died, it was his sister Mary who became queen. Poor Lady Jane went to the block, along with Northumberland.

MARY AND ELIZABETH

Elizabeth had become friends with Mary, who had taught her to play cards, but the two sisters were still divided by religion. Mary was a devout Catholic who dreamed of making England a Catholic country again. To this end she planned to marry Philip of Spain, the most devoutly Catholic prince in Europe.

▲ Lady Jane Grey was a member of the royal family. Her grandmother was Henry VIII's younger sister Mary.

The idea caused a rebellion, led by Sir Thomas Wyat. It failed but Mary was sure that Elizabeth knew of the plot against her, and sent her sister to the Tower of London. This was the most dangerous moment in Elizabeth's life so far.

EVENTS

1553 *Edward VI dies. Mary I becomes queen.*
1554 *Mary marries Philip of Spain. Wyat's rebellion fails.*
1555 *Elizabeth is allowed back to court. Protestant bishops Hugh Latimer and Nicholas Ridley are burned at the stake.*
1556 *Philip becomes king of Spain and the Netherlands.*
1558 *French recapture Calais, England's last possession in France. Mary I dies. Elizabeth becomes queen.*

▶ **Mary I married Philip of Spain because he would help restore the Catholic faith to England, but he soon came to dislike her and life in England. He preferred his sister-in-law to his wife.**

Though Wyat was put to death, she escaped the axe, and was banished from court to Woodstock, in Oxfordshire.

THE LORD'S DOING

Mary's harsh treatment of Protestants fuelled religious troubles in England, while her marriage brought neither happiness nor a child. Philip soon tired of his English wife, and returned to Spain. Rejected and miserable, Mary died, of cancer, on 17 November 1558. Elizabeth was at Hatfield when a messenger brought the news. Now she was queen. 'This is the Lord's doing; it is marvellous in our eyes,' she said, quoting from the Bible.

RELIGIOUS QUARRELS

THE Reformation split Europe's Christians. Reformers, known as Protestants, wanted change in the church. Catholics, led by the pope in Rome, feared a break-up of the Christian world. During the reigns of Edward and Mary, Catholics and Protestants were put to death for refusing to change sides. Mary begged her sister to come back to the 'true faith', but Elizabeth always avoided a direct answer. Mary died hoping England would once again be Catholic. Elizabeth wanted an end to religious quarrels. England had enemies enough abroad.

◀ Thomas Wyat, the son of a poet, led a rebellion against Mary. Under torture, he claimed Elizabeth was part of the plot, but denied this before he died.

▼ Fearing for her life, Elizabeth (inset) wrote to her sister to beg for mercy. Mary was furious and sent the princess to the Tower (shown here in a modern photo), but later accepted that she was innocent.

ENTRY TO THE TRAITORS GATE

■ ELIZABETH'S ENGLAND ■

PEOPLE REJOICED at their new queen. Elizabeth was 'born English', and most people were glad not to have a Spanish prince as their ruler. Her coronation took place on 15 January 1559, a date chosen with the help of the royal astrologer, John Dee.

BALANCE OF POWER

Clever though she was, Elizabeth had little experience of the court. She relied on her chief adviser, William Cecil, Lord Burghley, who was to remain her loyal servant for 40 years. Not everyone welcomed the new queen. Many Catholics believed that Henry's marriage to Anne Boleyn had been unlawful, and King Henry II of France said that Mary Stuart Queen of Scots (his daughter-in-law), was England's rightful queen. King Philip of Spain, though a Catholic, backed Elizabeth – because he would not side with France. The queen knew that she, and her small country, were walking a tightrope.

▶ At her coronation, Elizabeth wears the crown and holds an orb and sceptre, symbols of the monarch's authority and right to rule.

▲ William Cecil was a father figure for Elizabeth. He advised her and watched out for plots against her.

Tudor Fashion

ELIZABETH'S court was the centre of fashion. The queen and her ladies wore dresses decorated with pearls and jewels, with high collars and a wide skirt held up by a circular frame made of whalebone. The queen had over 250 dresses. Noblemen too wore fantastic clothes, with colourful stockings, padded trunks and doublets, ruffs and cloaks. A courtier was expected to be a swordsman and a singer, and to dance as well as he rode a horse. Poor people wore plain, hard-wearing clothes, while children wore smaller versions of adult clothes.

Royal Tours

London, with its royal palaces and Parliament, was the centre of government, but Elizabeth knew she had to show herself to the people, rich and poor. So she travelled about the kingdom, through towns and villages. She visited the grand houses of her dukes and earls, often travelling with as many as 400 wagons and a thousand followers. Each noble family who welcomed her had to feed all the queen's courtiers and servants. They also had to provide musical entertainment or a performance by 'players' (actors) and deer-hunting, before she moved on, leaving her hosts worn-out and considerably poorer.

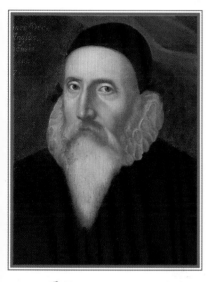

◀ John Dee was a serious scientist, as well as an astrologer and believer in magic.

▼ Elizabeth's vast retinue had to travel on roads that were dusty and bumpy in summer, and muddy or snow-covered in winter.

■ THE QUEEN'S COURTIERS ■

THE TUDOR court was like a huge family, made up of the queen's friends, attendants, advisers and hangers-on. Everyone at court took it for granted that Elizabeth would soon marry, to give the country an heir. There were many possible bridegrooms for the queen. Some were foreign princes, such as Philip, by now king of Spain. Elizabeth liked the French duke of Alençon, a short but gallant soldier who made her laugh, better than the gloomy Philip. By marrying a Spaniard, Elizabeth would make Spain a friend, but France an enemy. By keeping all her suitors guessing, the queen hoped to stop any foreign ruler taking control of her kingdom. Some English nobles also dreamed of gaining a crown by marriage.

▲ Elizabeth was fond of Robert Dudley. But he told the French ambassador that he had known Elizabeth since she was eight, and that she had always said she would never marry.

▼ Elizabeth, accompanied by her courtiers, is carried to Whitehall. Members of Parliament wanted a say in her choice of husband. She told them she was not the woman to have any man, or group of men, tell her what to do.

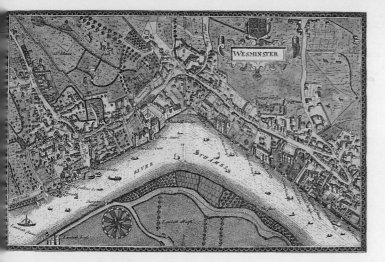

LONDON'S QUEEN

DURING Elizabeth's reign, London grew as the business centre of the country, and opened its first 'exchange'. Trade grew fast. New quays were built along the river Thames where ships could unload goods and be taxed. Only one bridge – London Bridge – crossed the river, further down from Westminster. It was packed end to end with houses and shops, and at its southern side stood inns for travellers. New vessels for the navy and for voyages of exploration were built at shipyards downriver. New industries included silk-weaving and glass-making.

ELIZABETHAN THEATRE

NEW theatres were built alongside the Thames. Here, late in Elizabeth's reign, William Shakespeare lived, acted and wrote his plays. Elizabeth enjoyed plays at court and had her own company of actors, the Queen's Men. All parts were taken by men, with boys or youths playing women and children. Shakespeare acted before the queen at Greenwich in 1594, and is supposed to have written *The Merry Wives of Windsor* at her request, so that she could see the character of Falstaff again in a new play.

▲ The duke of Alençon, Elizabeth's 'official' French suitor, was only half her age. She managed to stay friends with him, and with France, without marrying him.

SWEET ROBIN

In 1562 Elizabeth was seriously ill with smallpox. When she got better, she named her favourite English lord as Protector, to rule the land should she fall ill again. Her choice was Robert Dudley, son of the duke of Northumberland, whom the queen called her 'Eyes' and her 'sweet Robin'. Dudley, however, was already married, and when his wife died after falling downstairs, some at court whispered of scandal and murder.

In 1564 Elizabeth made Dudley earl of Leicester. She showered him with gifts but would not agree to marry him. She let other men make a play for her, including the clever Christopher Hatton, a fine dancer, and later the witty Walter Raleigh, who talked to her of voyages to America.

THE VIRGIN QUEEN

Elizabeth never married. She went on playing the 'marriage game' until 1583, when (aged 49) she told the duke of Alençon to give up and go home. Dudley had already given up hope of becoming king and married again in secret. He still held his place in the queen's heart, and when he died in 1588 she shut herself up in her room. She treasured his last letter to her, keeping it in a box with a note in her own handwriting.

■ PLOTS AND CONSPIRACIES ■

ENGLAND WAS growing richer from trade and from piracy. English sea captains, such as John Hawkins and Francis Drake, made raids on treasure-laden Spanish galleons returning from the Americas. Danger from abroad still haunted the queen. In 1570 the pope declared that Elizabeth was not England's lawful ruler. Later, he went further and said that to kill Elizabeth would not be a crime in the eyes of God.

THREATS TO ELIZABETH

Europe was split by religious wars. In the Netherlands, Spanish soldiers were fighting Dutch Protestants who had rebelled against Spanish rule. A large Spanish army across the North Sea was a constant threat to England, especially now that anti-Tudor plotters had the Catholic Church's backing to overthrow Elizabeth. The focus for these plots was

EVENTS

1559 Spain and France make peace.
1561 Mary Queen of Scots returns to Scotland after the death of her French husband, the king of France. Religious wars between Catholics and Protestants in France.
1568 Dutch Protestants revolt against Spanish rule.
1569 Northern rebellion against Elizabeth, led by Catholic nobles.
1571 Ridolfi plot against Elizabeth is uncovered. Battle of Lepanto between Turks and European allies.
1572 St Bartholomew's Day massacres in France; hundreds of Huguenots (French Protestants) are killed.

▲ Mary Stuart's life was turbulent and tragic. She was constantly involved in love affairs and plots. Because she and her supporters were Catholic, she posed a threat to Elizabeth.

▼ Francis Drake and his ship the *Golden Hind*. After three years at sea, finding new lands to trade with and attacking Spanish ships, he returned to a hero's welcome and a knighthood from the queen.

▼ During Elizabeth's reign, the Netherlands was ruled by Catholic Spain. Rebellions by Dutch Protestants were violently put down by the Spanish.

▲ Elizabeth ruled herself and her country wisely, showing more sense than her cousin Mary. She let no lover influence her and used the rule of law against her enemies.

▶ Sir Francis Walsingham kept his eyes and ears open for plots against the realm. His network of spies made up the Tudor secret service.

Mary Stuart, the Scottish queen, who was a Catholic. Her claim to the English throne was as the great-granddaughter of Henry VII.

In 1569, an uprising in northern England was led by Catholic lords who wanted to make Mary queen of England too. In 1571, an Italian banker named Roberto Ridolfi masterminded a new plot involving Mary, Catholic lords in England led by the duke of Norfolk, and the king of Spain. This was discovered by agents of Elizabeth's chief secretary, Francis Walsingham, whose job was to guard against spies. The plotters, including the duke of Norfolk, were arrested, tortured and executed.

TARGET: THE QUEEN

Elizabeth's advisers told her that Mary was central to all this plotting, but the queen held back from action, for fear of starting a war with Spain or France. She preferred to remain on guard, although the danger to her life was real. If a dagger or pistol were to end Elizabeth's life, the way would be open for Mary Stuart.

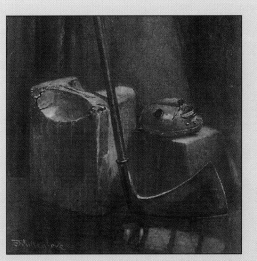

TUDOR TORMENTS

PUNISHMENTS in Tudor England were harsh and painful. Death was the penalty for plotting against the state. Nobles usually had their heads cut off with an axe, which was at least quick. Others found guilty of treason were hanged, drawn (disembowelled) and quartered (cut in four pieces). The thumbscrew, red-hot irons and the rack, which stretched the victim slowly, were a few of the torture instruments used to make suspects talk.

■ ELIZABETH AND MARY ■

ALTHOUGH Scotland's queen was Catholic, many Scots were Protestants. They were unhappy when Mary decided to take another husband. Her choice was Lord Darnley, her Catholic cousin. This upset the Protestant lords in Scotland. Mary gave birth to a son, James, but quickly discovered that Darnley was weak and worthless. In 1567 he was killed when his house was blown up. Mary then married the earl of Bothwell, an ambitious Scottish noble widely thought to have planned Darnley's murder.

The Scots would not have Bothwell as their 'king' and rose against Mary. She fled to England, giving up the throne to her baby son, who became King James VI of Scotland.

Elizabeth did not know what to do about Mary, who had powerful friends in Europe and was a queen like herself. For almost 20 years Mary was Elizabeth's 'guest', kept secure but comfortable as a prisoner in English castles. The two women, distant cousins, never met.

EVENTS

1567 Darnley dies in a mystery bomb-blast. Mary marries Bothwell, but is forced to leave Scotland.
1568 Mary flees to England.
1569 Northern Rebellion in support of Mary's claim to the throne of England.
1570 Turks attack Cyprus.
1571 Turks beaten at sea battle of Lepanto.
1572 Duke of Norfolk executed for plotting against Elizabeth.
1577 Akbar the Great rules northern India for the Moguls.
1586 Babington plot discovered.
1587 Mary is executed at Fotheringhay Castle.

▲ In 1567 Mary was forced to give up her throne to her baby son James.

▼ Mary sees the disastrous results of her battle to regain power in Scotland. Her defeat at Langside near Glasgow in 1568 left her no choice but to flee to England. There she had friends and much sympathy, even from Elizabeth, who in the end was reluctant to sign her cousin's death warrant.

PLOTS AFTER DINNER

MUCH of the plotting against Elizabeth would have taken place after the evening meal, at an inn or a feast in the great hall of a nobleman. Elizabeth herself was not a big eater, but many of her subjects liked a lot of meat – beef, mutton, pork, chicken, rabbit, deer and wild birds. Keeping to church tradition, everyone ate fish on Fridays. Vegetables were less popular. Rich diners washed down their food with wine from France. Poor people swigged down beakers of ale, cider or buttermilk. Even for a picnic (right) food was prepared in great quantities.

THE BABINGTON PLOT

Walsingham's spies kept watch on Mary and her friends, and read her letters. In 1586 a rich young Catholic called Anthony Babington became mixed up in yet another plot against Elizabeth. Believing that a Spanish army was ready to invade England, he told Mary that his friends would rally English supporters, remove Elizabeth, and make Mary queen. Walsingham's agents seized letters passing between Mary and Babington. Their contents sealed the fates of both.

Babington went on the run, but in August 1586 he was arrested, tried and put to death. Mary too was put on trial, in Fotheringhay Castle, and sentenced to death, but Elizabeth hesitated for three months before signing the death warrant. Six months after the execution, she ordered an impressive funeral for her dead 'sister-queen'.

▲ Elizabeth was no great beauty, but she dressed in magnificent clothes with a dazzling array of jewels.

▶ Mary, renowned for her beauty, stirred strong passions in friends and enemies, but she lacked her cousin's wisdom.

▶ Mary Stuart went to her death dressed in red, the colour for martyrs in Catholic ritual. After Mary was executed in February 1587, church bells rang out and people cheered. But Elizabeth raged at her servants, refused to see Burghley, and sent away food. The death of a queen on the executioner's block was an echo of her father's reign.

■ THE GREAT ARMADA ■

ENGLAND AND Spain were enemies, although not yet at war. In 1585 a small English army commanded by the earl of Leicester had joined the Dutch Protestants in their fight against the Catholic Spanish in the Netherlands. The death of Mary Queen of Scots now gave Spain's king Philip the excuse he needed to attack England. If he won and got rid of Elizabeth, he could make himself ruler of England and return its people to the Catholic Church.

KING PHILIP'S WAR

In 1586, Philip prepared a vast invasion fleet to send to England, but Sir Francis Drake led a daring attack on the Spanish port of Cadiz and destroyed many ships before they could sail. This delayed the fleet's start until 1588.

The Spanish plan was to sail up the English Channel, join the army of the duke of Parma in the Netherlands and cross the narrow sea to land in southern England. Philip believed many English

▲ Philip II was determined to teach Elizabeth and her pirates a lesson. He felt sure that God was on his side.

EVENTS

1562 Hawkins leads the first English slave-trading expedition.
1577-80 Francis Drake sails around the world, the second explorer to do so (after Magellan, 1519-22), and is knighted by Elizabeth in 1581.
1579 Spain tries to start an uprising of Irish Catholics against English control of Ireland, but it fails.
1580 Spain conquers Portugal.
1581 Dutch found a republic, following years of fighting against Spanish rule.
1585 English army fights in the Netherlands, against Spain, without much success.
1587 Mary Queen of Scots is executed (February).
1588 Armada sails in July.

SEA DOGS

ENGLISH sailors – 'sea dogs' – were admired and feared. Among the first was Sir John Hawkins who made the first English slaving voyage to Africa. The most famous was Francis Drake, who sailed round the world. Walter Raleigh (left) was a favourite of the queen. He made the first English voyage to America, and named Virginia for her. Having conquered an empire in South America, Spain controlled trade with the New World, and regarded the English as criminal intruders. When English ships attacked Spanish ships, the king of Spain protested but Elizabeth replied there was little she could do. Raiding the Spanish brought her rich rewards.

would join his 'holy war' and remove Elizabeth. In fact, most English Catholics were loyal to their queen.

THE SPANISH ARE COMING

The English knew that the Spanish were coming. The queen's cousin, Lord Howard of Effingham, commanded the English fleet against the duke of Medina Sidonia who commanded the great Armada for Spain. At Howard's side were Drake, Frobisher, Hawkins and other captains with years of sea-fighting experience and local knowledge of winds and tides. The English plan was to keep the Armada from landing, for a land battle would probably mean Spanish victory.

The Armada was sighted on 29 July. Warning beacons were lit along the coasts of England. Forts were manned, cannon prepared and ships set sail. When the Armada reached Calais, in France, the English attacked with fireships, and the next day the two fleets fought a battle with no clear winner.

▼ The Spanish fleet was the largest that had ever put to sea. It included towering galleons, and galleases and galleys (ships with oars as well as sails). Thousands of men were to lose their lives in the battle that followed.

■ ELIZABETH TRIUMPHANT ■

ON 18 AUGUST, Elizabeth rode down to Tilbury in Essex. Dressed in white velvet with a shining silver breastplate and mounted on her horse, she roused the waiting soldiers with an inspiring speech, promising to live or die with them in any battle to come.

By then, the Spanish Armada was far away, its battle plans thwarted by the weather. High winds drove the fleet north, away from southern England and along the east coast towards Scotland. Storms

EVENTS

1588 *Armada fails to meet the duke of Parma's army in the Netherlands and is beaten by English ships and the weather. Survivors reach Spain in September 1588.*
1589 *Protestant Henri of Navarre becomes king of France.*
1596 *Francis Drake dies of dysentery while raiding Spanish bases in Central America.*

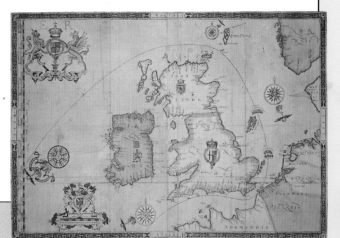

SHIPS OF THE ARMADA

THE English had 197 ships, more than the 130 of the Armada, but most of them were smaller than the Spaniards'. The biggest was Frobisher's *Triumph*, an old ship of 1100 tonnes. Drake fought in the *Revenge* (bottom), half the size, but fast and heavily armed with cannon. The Spanish ships were a mix of slow-moving transports and giant galleons, loaded with troops, guns and stores. Their crews fought bravely, but the English could sail faster, turn quicker, and fire their guns at a much faster rate.

◀ **The map shows the course of the battle, through the English Channel and into the North Sea. On the voyage home, many Spanish ships sank, and more than 10,000 Spanish soldiers and sailors perished.**

dashed many ships onto rocks as the Armada struggled to sail round the British Isles. Fewer than half its ships got home to Spain. For Philip of Spain it was a disaster: for Elizabeth's England a glorious victory.

ENGLAND IS SAFE

The failure of the Armada put fresh heart into the Protestants of Europe. Elizabeth was now safe as queen of England. Although England and Spain went on fighting until 1604, a year after her death, England was never so seriously in danger again.

▼ Soldiers cheered as Elizabeth addressed the troops assembled at Tilbury. She told them 'we shall shortly have a famous victory over these enemies of my God, my kingdom, and of my people'.

TRADE AND MONEY

WHEN Elizabeth became queen, England had severe money problems. Her father and brother had 'debased' the coins, mixing gold with cheap metal so that most were worth less than their face value. Foreign traders refused to accept English money, demanding gold instead. In 1560, Cecil 'revalued' English money, so that overnight six pennies became worth only four pennies. London's goldsmiths melted down old coins to separate the gold and silver from the cheaper metals. Elizabeth visited the Royal Mint in the Tower of London, and made several new coins herself, including the 'crown' (above).

■ A LONELY OLD AGE ■

ELIZABETH WAS triumphant. England surged with new confidence and energy, but the queen herself was feeling tired and sad. She was losing her dearest friends. Walsingham died in 1590, Christopher Hatton in 1591, Drake in 1596, and in 1598 Burghley, at the age of 78. She took comfort in the lively company of young Robert Devereux, earl of Essex. He was Leicester's stepson, and had fought bravely at Cadiz in 1596. He was also excitable and boastful, quite the opposite of Elizabeth's new chief minister, Robert Cecil, son of Lord Burghley.

IRELAND AND ESSEX

Ireland was ruled by England, but not well. Most Irish people were Catholics, and so were treated as likely enemies, possible allies of Spain. In 1598 the earl of Tyrone led an Irish rebellion. An army would have to be sent to deal with the rebels, and Essex begged to lead it. Against her better judgement, Elizabeth agreed.

Essex was a failure. His army tramped about Ireland without winning a battle, and when he came home, he was arrested for disobeying orders. He was freed, but the queen would not see him. He then foolishly attempted a rebellion of his own, marching through London with about 200 followers. The citizens refused to join him. He was arrested again,

EVENTS

1591 *Elizabeth founds Trinity College, Dublin.*
1595 *Walter Raleigh sails to South America in search of El Dorado, the mythical land of gold.*
1596 *English attack the Spanish port of Cadiz, to prevent a second invasion setting sail.*
1598 *Rebellion in Ireland against English rule. Edict of Nantes ends religious wars in France.*
1600 *Beginning of Tokugawa rule in Japan.*
1601 *Earl of Essex executed. New Poor Law makes parishes responsible for the poor.*
1603 *Elizabeth dies and is succeeded by James VI of Scotland, son of Mary Queen of Scots.*

and this time there was no escape. He was executed for treason early in 1601. Elizabeth was sad, but resigned; 'I had warned him . . .' she told the French ambassador.

FAREWELL TO PARLIAMENT

Elizabeth's last years were lonely. She hated looking old, and wore a reddish wig over her thinning hair, and rather too much make-up on her face. After Essex's death, she spoke to her members of Parliament for the last time. 'Though God has raised me high,' she said, 'yet this I count the glory of my crown, that I have reigned with your love'.

▼ The earl of Essex was as handsome and dashing as his stepfather, Robert Dudley, but alas not as loyal.

MUSIC AND SONG

QUEEN Elizabeth loved music as much as plays. She danced with great vigour, and gave royal support to church music, protecting it from Puritans who thought music-making in church was sinful. Thomas Tallis (about 1510-1585) and William Byrd (1543-1623), who played the organ in the queen's chapel, composed some of England's greatest church music. Foreigners much admired the singing of the men and boys of the Chapel Royal. The queen's support was gratefully received: 'If it were not the Queen's Majesty did favour that excellent science, singing men and choristers might go a-begging'.

◀ Portrayed as Gloriana, the greatest woman of the age, Elizabeth stands on the map of her kingdom which, she said, may have had 'many princes more mighty and wise' but which 'never had, or shall have, any that will be more careful and loving'.

■ THE TUDOR LEGACY ■

THERE WERE no more Tudors to sit on England's throne. As the queen's life neared its end, Cecil and the English lords were already exchanging coded messages with Scotland. James VI, son of Mary Queen of Scots, waited to be king, knowing he was Elizabeth's heir, though she never actually named him.

A SCOTTISH HEIR

After a cheerful Whitehall Christmas in 1602, the queen moved to her palace at Richmond. At the end of February she became ill. She ate nothing, slept little and sat on the floor without speaking. Persuaded to take to her bed, Elizabeth died on 24 March 1603. Fast horses bore the government messenger to

▼ Elizabeth's funeral (bottom) and her tomb in Westminster Abbey. She was genuinely mourned by her people, and her reign is remembered as among the greatest in British history.

The Chariott drawne by foure Horses upon which Charret stood the Coffin covered with purple Veluett and upon that the representation, The Canapy borne by six Knights.

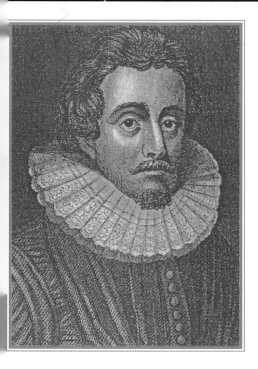

▲ James I never commanded the loyalty that the people showed to Elizabeth nor earned their love.

Scotland, where he greeted James with his new title: 'King of England, Scotland, France and Ireland'.

Elizabeth's last journey was from Richmond to Whitehall by river boat. Her funeral was an impressive parade, headed by 240 poor women and escorted by lords and soldiers. Her coffin lay on a carriage drawn by four horses in black velvet. She was buried in Westminster Abbey next to her grandfather, Henry VII – the first and last Tudor monarchs together.

A GOLDEN AGE

People soon spoke of Elizabeth's reign as a golden age, when England changed from a weak and divided nation into a country richer and more united, with the first seeds of its overseas empire already planted. They remembered the many great people of Elizabeth's age, from poets to pirates.

Elizabeth died knowing that she had done what she could to see that her people should 'live in a flourishing and happy condition'. She loved her nation and subjects, and most of them returned her affection and remembered her as the greatest of all the Tudors.

footemen

■ GLOSSARY ■

AGENT Person working in secret for a government, as a spy, or for the secret police.

AMBASSADOR Official sent abroad to pass messages between his home country and that to which he has been sent.

ARCHBISHOP A senior bishop in the Church; the archbishop of Canterbury is the senior churchman of the Church of England.

ARMADA Spanish war-fleet sent to invade England.

ASSASSINATION Murder of a leader or some important person.

ASTROLOGER Someone who believes the stars guide people's fates.

BLOCK Piece of wood on which someone about to be beheaded rested his or her head.

CANNON Metal gun firing a solid iron ball.

CATHOLIC In Christian religion, a person belonging to the Catholic Church, headed by the pope in Rome.

COCK-FIGHTING Cruel 'sport' in which cockerels (male chickens) were put to fight one another in a small ring. Spectators took bets on the winner.

COURT The establishment (buildings and people) around a king or queen.

COURTIER Member of a king's or queen's court, usually a noble.

DISEMBOWEL To 'draw' out the bowels, or innards, of an animal. In Tudor times hanged men were 'drawn' while still half alive.

DYSENTERY Sickness affecting the stomach and bowels, leading to death if not properly treated.

EAST INDIA COMPANY Trading company formed to send ships to Asia, especially the East Indies (Indonesia).

EXCHANGE Marketplace for money and shares in business ventures.

EXECUTION Killing of a person found guilty of a serious crime.

FALCON Bird of prey, trained in the sport of falconry, or hawking, to hunt other birds and small animals.

FIRESHIP Ship set on fire, then set to drift in among enemy ships at anchor.

GALLEON Large sailing ship, first used in Tudor times.

GRAMMAR SCHOOL Boys' school in Tudor England, where Latin grammar was taught, and from which many later schools evolved.

HOUSE (family) Name used for a royal family, such as the House of York, House of Stuart.

HUGUENOTS French Protestants, some of whom sought refuge in England from religious persecution.

ILLEGITIMATE Outside the law, often describing a child born to unmarried parents.

LATIN Language of Ancient Romans, still used in Europe in the 1500s.

LUTE Stringed instrument, similar to a guitar.

MOGULS Muslim people who founded an empire in India in the early 1500s.

MONARCH A king or queen.

PLAGUE Highly infectious disease that wiped out thousands of people.

POPE Leader of the Catholic Church in Rome.

PROTECTOR Someone acting as stand-in ruler until a child king or queen grows up.

PROTESTANT Supporter of the Reformation, which led to the establishment of new churches with teachings and worship different from those of the Roman Catholic Church.

PURITANS Christians in England who practised a simple form of worship, disapproved of the theatre, and wore plain, dark clothing.

QUAY Loading and unloading area for ships on a river bank or in a harbour.

REBELLION Uprising by people who wish to get rid of a government they do not like.

REFORMATION Religious movement for change, also known as Protestantism, begun in Germany by Martin Luther, which challenged the power of the Catholic Church.

RENAISSANCE New birth, period from the 14th century when scholars and artists in western Europe gained inspiration from rediscovered works of the ancient Greeks and Romans.

RETINUE People following a queen or some other important person as he or she travels around.

ROYAL MINT Factory where coins are made, and stamped with the monarch's head.

RUFF Frill, usually pleated into folds, worn like a collar in Elizabethan times.

SLAVE TRADE The buying and selling of people who were held captive and forced to work for their owners.

SMALLPOX Infectious disease that caused scarring of the face, and could kill. It was much feared in Elizabethan times.

STUART Family name of the dynasty, or royal line, to which Mary Queen of Scots and her son James I of England belonged.

SUCCEED To follow, especially to inherit the throne when the king or queen dies.

SUITOR A man wishing to marry a woman.

TORTURE Hurting someone to make them tell a secret or confess to a crime.

TOURNAMENT Competition in which knights on horseback fought with blunted lances and swords, to show off their skill with weapons.

TRAITOR Person guilty of the crime of treason.

TREASON Plotting to remove, harm or kill the rightful ruler of a country.

TUBERCULOSIS Serious disease affecting the lungs.

TUDOR Family name of the dynasty, or royal line, to which Elizabeth I belonged, founded by Henry VII.

TUTOR Private teacher, employed to teach children at home.

VIRGINALS Early keyboard musical instrument.

WARS OF THE ROSES Civil wars in England between the royal families of Lancaster and York, from which Henry Tudor emerged victorious in 1485.

WHITEHALL Royal palace in London, known as York Place before Elizabeth's father, Henry VIII, had it rebuilt.

PLACES TO VISIT

Buckland Abbey
Yelverton, Devon
Sir Francis Drake's home

Burghley House
Stamford, Lincolnshire
Home of the Cecil family

Hardwick Hall
near Chesterfield, Derbyshire
Home of Bess of Hardwick, one of the great women of Elizabeth's age

Hatfield House
Hertfordshire
Part of the royal palace where Elizabeth lived as a child still remains

Hever Castle
Kent
Home of Elizabeth's mother, Anne Boleyn

National Portrait Gallery
London
Many paintings of Elizabethan men and women

National Maritime Museum
Greenwich, London
Exhibits of Tudor ships and exploration

Westminster Abbey
London
Tombs of Elizabeth and Mary Queen of Scots

The Tower of London
London
Fortress where prisoners were taken to be executed

■ INDEX ■